CIVIL WAR CHRONICLES

LINCOLN

By Ruth Ashby

A⁺

For Ernie   —R.A.

Published by Smart Apple Media
1980 Lookout Drive, North Mankato, Minnesota 56003

Produced by Byron Preiss Visual Publications, Inc.

Library of Congress Cataloging-in-Publication Data
Ashby, Ruth.
Lincoln / by Ruth Ashby
v. cm. — (Civil War chronicles)
Contents: Beginnings — Politics — Commander in Chief — The Lincoln White
House — The scourge of war — Now he belongs to the ages.
ISBN 1-58340-183-0
1. Lincoln, Abraham, 1809-1865—Juvenile literature. 2. Presidents—United States—
Biography—Juvenile literature. [1. Lincoln, Abraham, 1809-1865 2. Presidents.]
I. Title.

E457.905 .A84 2002
973.7'092—dc21   2002017647
[B]

First Edition
9 8 7 6 5 4 3 2 1

Contents

Introduction

The Civil War was the great American tragedy. From 1861 to 1865, it divided states, broke up families, took the lives of more than half a million people, and left much of the country in ruins. But it also abolished the great national shame of slavery and cleared the way for the astounding expansion of American industry and culture in the second half of the 19th century. Without the war, the United States would not have been so progressive or so united—and millions of its people would still have been in chains. In the end it was, perhaps, a necessary tragedy.

The conflict had loomed for decades. From the Constitutional Convention in 1787 on, the North and South disagreed about whether slavery should exist in the United States. In the North, slavery was gradually abolished between 1780 and 1827. But the South became ever more yoked to slavery as its economy became more dependent on the production of cotton. In the meantime, the United States was expanding westward. Every time a territory became a new state, the government had to decide whether it would be slave or free. For 40 years, Congress reached compromise after compromise.

Finally, differences could no longer be bandaged over. With the election of Republican Abraham Lincoln to the presidency in 1860, a crisis was reached. Southern states were afraid that Lincoln, who opposed slavery in the territories, would try to abolish it in the South as well—and that their economy and way of life would be destroyed. On December 20, 1860, South Carolina seceded from the Union. It was

⊠ Abraham Lincoln

⊠ Jefferson Davis

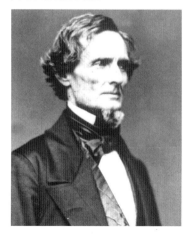

Robert E. Lee ✠

Ulysses S. Grant ✠

followed by Alabama, Florida, Georgia, Louisiana, Mississippi, Texas, Virginia, North Carolina, Tennessee, and Arkansas.

The rebellious states formed a new nation, the Confederate States of America, and elected a president, Jefferson Davis. On April 12, 1861, Confederate forces fired on the Federal post of Fort Sumter in Charleston Harbor—and the Civil War began. It lasted four years and touched the lives of every man, woman, and child in the nation. There were heroes on both sides, in the army and on the home front, from Union general Ulysses S. Grant and Confederate general Robert E. Lee to black leader Harriet Tubman and poet and nurse Walt Whitman. It is estimated that at least 620,000 soldiers were killed, almost as many Americans as in all other armed conflicts combined. When Lincoln issued the Emancipation Proclamation on January 1, 1863, and freed the slaves in the rebellious states, it became not just a war for reunification but a war of liberation as well.

Lincoln chronicles the extraordinary life of the man who held the nation together during the most perilous years of its history—and who, like millions of his countrymen, eventually gave his life so that a "government of the people, by the people, for the people, shall not perish from the earth."

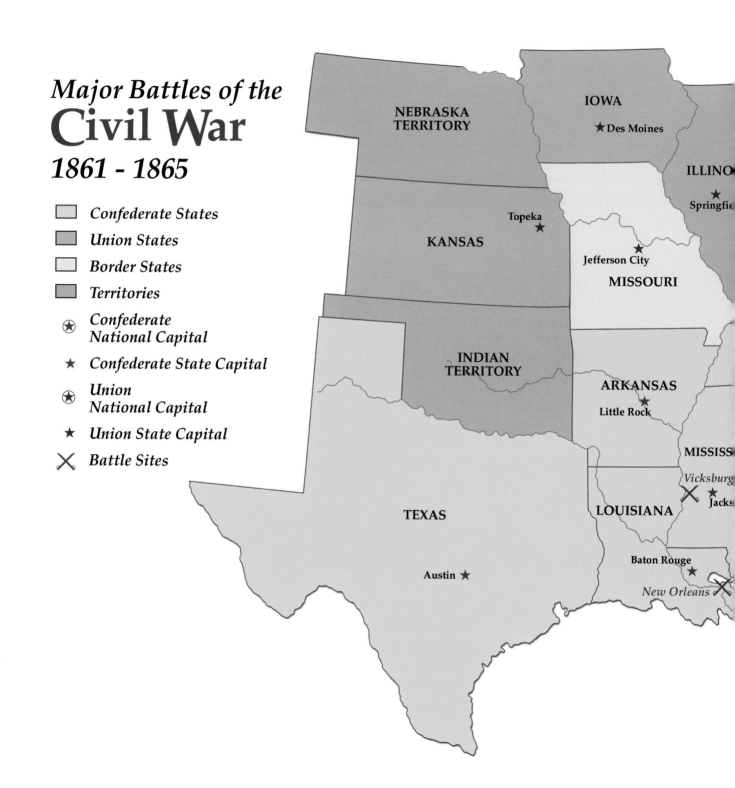

Major Battles of the
Civil War
1861 - 1865

Confederate States

Union States

Border States

Territories

⊛ Confederate
National Capital

★ Confederate State Capital

⊛ Union
National Capital

★ Union State Capital

✕ Battle Sites

NEBRASKA
TERRITORY

IOWA

★ Des Moines

ILLINO

★
Springfie

Topeka ★

KANSAS

★
Jefferson City

MISSOURI

INDIAN
TERRITORY

ARKANSAS

★
Little Rock

MISSISS

TEXAS

LOUISIANA

Vicksburg

✕ ★ Jacks

Baton Rouge
★

Austin ★

New Orleans ✕

BATTLES (on map below)

1 *Gettysburg*
2 *Antietam*
3 *Shenandoah Campaign*
4 *First and Second Manassas*
5 *Wilderness*
6 *Fredericksburg*
7 *Spotsylvania*
8 *Chancellorsville*
9 *Cold Harbor*
10 *Seven Days' Battles*
11 *Petersburg*
12 *Peninsular Campaign*
13 *First and Second Hampton Roads*

Quick Facts

★ Kentucky, where Abraham was born, was a slaveholding state. The Baptist church the Lincolns attended was bitterly divided between people who approved of slavery and people who didn't. Thomas Lincoln was among those who thought slavery was wrong. One of the reasons he moved his family to Indiana was because it was a free state.

★ The kind of school Lincoln attended was called a "blab" school. All the students recited their lessons out loud at the same time.

★ Lincoln wrote a letter to the editor of a local paper when he was running for office in 1836: "Every man is said to have his peculiar ambition. . . . I have no other so great as that of being esteemed of my fellow men, by rendering myself worthy of their esteem."

⊠ Abraham Lincoln, June 1860. Of this photograph, Lincoln said, "It looks better and expresses me better than any I have ever seen."

Chapter One

Beginnings

Abraham Lincoln was one of the most hated men in American history. His critics called him "a tyrant," "a backwoods president," "a Lincolnpoop," and "the Illinois ape." He guided the nation through its greatest trial, the American Civil War, when hundreds of thousands of men—from Maine to Mississippi, Tennessee to Texas—were killed. Many people thought Lincoln was directly to blame for the slaughter. But by the time he died, they understood how fortunate the country had been to have him as a president. Lincoln was the right man for the job, as black leader Frederick Douglass understood: "His greatest mission was to accomplish two things: first, to save his country from dismemberment and ruin; and second, to free his country from the great crime of slavery. . . . infinite wisdom has seldom sent any man into the world better fitted for his mission than Abraham Lincoln."

Lincoln was born on February 12, 1809, in a one-room log cabin in Kentucky. He was the only son of Thomas Lincoln, an illiterate carpenter and farmer, and Nancy Hanks Lincoln. Many American politicians have said they were of humble birth, the better to emphasize their rags-to-riches careers. President William Henry Harrison, for instance, claimed to have been born in a log cabin, even though he actually hailed from a large estate in Virginia. But Lincoln was a genuine "man of the people." His early life, he later told a reporter, could be summed up by

Lincoln at age 37. This is the earliest known photograph of Lincoln, taken in 1846 when he was a Springfield lawyer.

a line in Thomas Gray's famous "Elegy Written in a Country Churchyard": "the short and simple annals of the poor."

Work on the farm was unceasing and backbreaking. For Nancy, it was a dawn-to-dusk routine of cooking, cleaning, washing, sewing, and, of course, raising Abraham and his sister, Sarah. For Thomas, it involved endless planting and harvesting. In search of better farmland, Thomas moved his family across the Ohio River to the new state of Indiana when Abraham was seven. There the cycle of clearing the land, building a cabin, and planting crops began all over again.

When Abraham was nine, his mother died of milk sickness, a fever brought on by drinking the poisoned milk of cows. After struggling to get by in a womanless household, his father went back to Kentucky to bring back a new wife, the widow Sarah Johnson, and her three children. Sarah took Abe and his sister into her heart. Later Abe spoke of her as "a good and kind mother."

Abe was a sensitive child who hated to see anything hurt. Friends later remembered that he would climb a tree to put baby birds back in their nests. He shot a turkey once and was so upset he never shot at anything live again. As he grew older, the tall, gangly boy became a natural woodsman. "You'd have thought there was two men in the woods when he got into it with an ax," a friend recalled.

It was his love of reading that really set Abraham apart. He got his schooling here and there—by "littles," as he later quipped: a few days or weeks before planting or after harvesting. Lincoln wrote that all of his schooling together "did not amount to one year." But somehow he learned "readin', and writin', and cipherin'."

He read the family Bible. And he borrowed books from everyone he met: the plays of Shakespeare, Daniel Defoe's *Robinson Crusoe*, John Bunyan's *Pilgrim's Progress*, and *The Autobiography of Benjamin*

A sketch of young Abraham Lincoln ferrying people on a flatboat.

Franklin. One of his favorites was "Parson" Weems's inspirational *Life of George Washington*. Washington and the Founding Fathers became his heroes. "I have never had a feeling politically that did not spring from the sentiments of the Declaration of Independence," Lincoln said later.

By the time he was 17 years old, Abraham was the tallest (six feet four inches [193 cm]) and strongest young man around. He could hold an ax straight out by the handle and pick up a chicken house and move it by himself. He worked at dozens of odd jobs—splitting rails, sawing lumber, butchering, and clerking in a store. Once he built a ferryboat and ferried people across the river—before he was fined for not having a license.

Soon after, he got his first chance to leave home. With a friend, he took a flatboat loaded with farm goods down the Ohio and Mississippi Rivers to New Orleans. This cosmopolitan city of 44,000 was the busiest port west of the Atlantic Ocean. The country boys marveled at the crowds of sailors, traders, and townspeople speaking French, Spanish, and Portuguese. Lincoln saw his first theaters—and his first slave auctions. New Orleans had more than 200 slave dealers in 1829.

When he got home to Indiana, Abraham handed his father the $24 he had earned. Then he thought about his future. What did he want to do with his life? He was strong, able, and good with his hands. But he was also a natural storyteller and a gifted speaker. Lincoln decided he wanted to work with his mind. He'd had enough of hard physical labor. So he helped his family get settled in yet another farmstead—this time in Illinois—and declared his freedom. At age 22, Abraham Lincoln left home to become a clerk in a dry-goods store in New Salem, Illinois.

His friendliness and intelligence soon won people over. Over the course of the next six years, Lincoln joined a debating society, studied grammar and American history, became a surveyor and a postmaster, and ran for political office. He had his only brief military experience in the Black Hawk War, in which, as he recounted, he saw no action but "had a good many bloody struggles with mosquitoes." He opened his own grocery store with a partner who proceeded to drink all the profits away—and then died and left Lincoln to pay the bills. It took Lincoln 10 years to pay off the "National Debt," as he called it.

In the early 19th century, politics offered a quick way for a man to make a name for himself. In 1834, Lincoln ran for state legislature and won. But he still had to earn a living, since representatives earned their $3 a day only when the legislature was in session. Lincoln took the advice of a Springfield lawyer, John T. Stuart, and started to study law on his own. (Becoming a lawyer was an informal affair in those days.) Lincoln passed the bar exam in 1836. As luck would have it, the new state capital moved to Springfield that very year, and Lincoln became a

Mary Todd Lincoln at age 28. ⊠ This portrait is a companion to the photograph of her husband on page 9. Lincoln later said of the photographs, "They are very precious to me, taken when we were young and so desperately in love."

junior partner in Stuart's law firm.

When Lincoln rode into Springfield on a borrowed horse, he was just 28 years old and practically penniless. But he was in just the kind of place—a new state capital in a brand-new state—for an ambitious young man to make his mark. He was also in a town with an active social life, so he could meet eligible young women. In December 1839, Lincoln was introduced to 21-year-old Mary Todd , the spoiled daughter of a wealthy Kentucky banker. Pretty, plump, and vivacious, Mary was immediately drawn to the unpolished young lawyer. She told a friend he had "the most congenial mind" she'd ever met. The two fell head over heels in love. A year later, they were engaged.

Her family objected strongly to the match. In their eyes, Lincoln was a rough backwoodsman with plenty of ambition but no connections and no money. Mary stood up to them, but Lincoln, humiliated, broke off the engagement.

He plunged into depression. "I am now the most miserable man living," Lincoln wrote to Stuart. His roommate even hid his razor so that he wouldn't slit his own throat. It was 15 months before a friend arranged for Mary and Abraham to meet again. Immediately they realized they must marry. They announced their decision to her family on November 4, 1842. The wedding was held that very evening.

A short time later Lincoln wrote to a friend, "Nothing new here, except my marrying, which to me is a matter of profound wonder."

Chapter Two

The First Citizen of Springfield

Lincoln settled nicely into family life. His son Robert was born in 1843, just nine months after the wedding. Soon after, Lincoln bought his first and only house, a comfortable frame dwelling on a main street in Springfield. There, Mary gave birth to three more sons: Edward (1846), William (1850), and Thomas (1853), whom the family nicknamed Tad. (Eddie died in 1850, before he was four.)

The Lincolns' life in Springfield would be interrupted only once in the next 17 years. In 1846, Lincoln ran for Congress on the Whig

⌧ The street in Springfield where Lincoln had an office with his law partner, William Herndon. The office was on the right, in the last building on the block.

Quick Facts

★ Lincoln was known as "Honest Abe" for his scrupulous business practices. If he thought he had been overpaid, he was actually known to return fees. He once wrote some advice for young lawyers: "If in your own judgment, you cannot be an honest lawyer, resolve to be honest without being a lawyer."

★ Lincoln first met Stephen Douglas in Springfield, where they were both young lawyers and rivals for the hand of Mary Todd. When Douglas proposed to Mary, she rejected him, saying, "I can't consent to be your wife. I shall become Mrs. President . . . but it will not be as Mrs. Douglas."

★ In the election of 1860, Lincoln received 1,866,000 votes. Douglas, running on the Democratic ticket, had 1,377,000, and Breckinridge, the Southern Democrat, had 850,000. Although he won just 40 percent of the popular vote, Lincoln won the Electoral College, 180 to Douglas's 12.

★ During the presidential race, Lincoln received a letter from an 11-year-old girl named Grace Bedell, who suggested he grow a beard. "You would look a great deal better for your face is so thin," she explained. About a month later, he took her advice.

ticket and won a seat in the House of Representatives. He moved the family to Washington, D.C., for the duration of his term, though Mary soon got bored and left to spend time with her family in Kentucky.

Lincoln, meanwhile, had his first experience in national politics. It was not a success. The United States had just gone to war against Mexico and Lincoln disapproved. He called the war "immoral and unnecessary." But Illinois supported it, and Lincoln's position was unpopular. The Whigs did not invite him to run for a second term.

His political life at a standstill, Lincoln went back to Springfield to practice law. A few years earlier, he had opened his own office with partner William Herndon. Now he traveled the Illinois circuit, arguing tax, debt, rape, and murder cases. Soon Lincoln was one of the most sought-after lawyers in the state. He was a brilliant courtroom attorney. Juries were persuaded by his clear, compact arguments and entertained by his homespun humor. Adversaries lulled by his slow manner soon learned not to underestimate him. A colleague remembered, "Any man who took Lincoln for a simple-minded man would very soon wake up with his back in a ditch."

Lincoln was doing so well in private practice that he stayed out of politics for a while. But when Congress passed the Kansas-Nebraska Act in 1854, he was roused to action. The act declared that the citizens of Kansas and Nebraska would vote on whether the territories would be slave or free. It contradicted the Missouri Compromise of 1820, which had forbidden slavery in these territories. Lincoln, like many people, had thought that slavery would die a natural death. Now it looked as if it wouldn't.

Lincoln hated slavery. In his view, it was not only immoral and un-Christian, it was un-American. Slavery denied blacks the rights given to free citizens of the nation. A few years later, when he was running for president, Lincoln told a group in New Haven, "I am not ashamed to confess that 25 years ago I was a hired laborer, mauling rails, at work on a flatboat—just what might [have] happened to any poor man's son. I want every man to have a chance—and I believe a black man is entitled to it—in which he can better his condition." But Lincoln was no abolitionist. Abolitionists, in his opinion, were fanatics who would break the law and "burn the last copy of the Bible rather than slavery continue a single hour."

Because of the act, the "monstrous injustice" of slavery would spread. Not only that, but the sponsor of the bill, Stephen Douglas, was actually the Democratic senator from Illinois. Lincoln gave speeches across the state. "As I would not be a slave, so I would not be a master," Lincoln told his audiences. "This expresses my idea of democracy." He joined the new Republican Party, dedicated to controlling slavery. And he ran for office again.

Lincoln failed to win a senate seat as a Whig in 1855. But then Republicans nominated him to oppose Douglas in the election of 1858. Lincoln gave a stirring speech before the Republican State Convention in Springfield, Illinois. "'A house divided against itself cannot stand,'" he said, quoting the Bible. "I believe this government cannot endure, permanently half slave and half free. . . . It will become all one thing, or all the other." Lincoln would do everything in his power to make sure it became free.

That summer and fall, the Lincoln-Douglas debates electrified the nation. "The prairies are on fire," one New York reporter wrote. The two candidates made quite a study in contrasts. The sturdy Douglas was a full foot (30 cm) shorter than Lincoln, with an aggressive manner and a loud, booming voice. Lincoln, tall and gawky, had a high voice and a rural Kentucky twang. The press called them the "Little Giant" and

✉ Stephen A. Douglas, the "Little Giant." Douglas was responsible for the passage of the Kansas-Nebraska Act, which threatened to allow slavery in the western territories.

Crowds gather at Knox College in Illinois, on October 7, 1858, for the fifth of seven Lincoln-Douglas debates. Citizens welcomed the candidates to town with marching bands and barbecues.

"Long Abe." Douglas defended "popular sovereignty"—the right of each state to decide on slavery for itself. Lincoln argued that slavery was a moral issue for all Americans to decide as a nation.

Douglas won the election. "I am too big to cry, and too badly hurt to laugh," Lincoln admitted to a friend afterward. But the debates had put Long Abe in the national spotlight. He went on a whirlwind speaking tour throughout the Northern states. Soon there was talk of his running for president. "The taste *is* in my mouth a little," he had to confess. Sure enough, Illinois's favorite son was nominated for president at the Republican National Convention in May 1860.

In those days, presidential candidates usually did not go out on the campaign trail themselves. So Lincoln remained in Springfield while his supporters held rallies for "Honest Abe," and Republican crowds sang the popular campaign song "Old Abe Lincoln Came Out of the Wilderness." On Election Day, Lincoln camped out in the telegraph office until all the returns came in. When victory was certain, he told his supporters, "Well, boys, your troubles are over now, but mine have just begun." At 2:00 A.M. he woke up his wife. "Mary," he said, "we are elected!"

The South erupted in a frenzy. A "Black Republican" had been elected to the White House, and Southerners felt that their property and their homes—even their honor—were threatened. "The evil days . . . are upon us," warned the *Dallas Herald*. "The South should arm at once!" blared the *Augusta Constitutionalist*.

Soon, it did.

Chapter Three

Commander in Chief

Just six weeks after Lincoln's election, South Carolina seceded from the Union. Over the next month and a half, Mississippi, Florida, Alabama, Georgia, Louisiana, and Texas followed. Lincoln could only watch helplessly as lame-duck president James Buchanan threw up his hands

The first inauguration of Abraham Lincoln on March 4, 1861. The incomplete dome of the U.S. Capitol rises behind him.

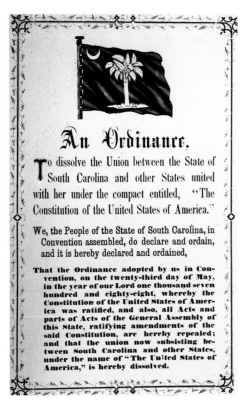

An Ordinance,

To dissolve the Union between the State of South Carolina and other States united with her under the compact entitled, "The Constitution of the United States of America."

We, the People of the State of South Carolina, in Convention assembled, do declare and ordain, and it is hereby declared and ordained,

That the Ordinance adopted by us in Convention, on the twenty-third day of May, in the year of our Lord one thousand seven hundred and eighty-eight, whereby the Constitution of the United States of America was ratified, and also, all Acts and parts of Acts of the General Assembly of this State, ratifying amendments of the said Constitution, are hereby repealed; and that the union now subsisting between South Carolina and other States, under the name of "The United States of America," is hereby dissolved.

The Ordinance of Secession ✠ signed by South Carolina delegates on December 22, 1860.

✠ (opposite): Fort Sumter during the bombardment. Confederate guns opened fire on the Federal fort at 4:30 A.M. on April 12, 1861.

and did nothing. As Inauguration Day neared, rumors of treason and sabotage grew. During his train journey from Illinois to Washington, Lincoln was rushed secretly from city to city because his staff feared an assassination plot.

Lincoln's inaugural address on March 4, 1861, was a deliberate attempt to ward off a conflict between the North and the South. He assured Southerners that the government would neither attack them nor interfere with the institution of slavery where it already existed. And he asked secessionists to remember the common history that linked all the United States together, so that "the mystic chords of memory, stretching from every battlefield and patriot grave to every living heart and hearthstone all over this broad land, will yet swell the chorus of the Union, when again touched, as surely they will be, by the better angels of our nature."

Already Lincoln had a crisis on his hands. On March 5, he learned that the Confederacy had demanded the surrender of Fort Sumter, a U.S. Army fort in Charleston Harbor. Its commander, Major Robert Anderson, told Lincoln he would run out of supplies in a month. Lincoln decided to resupply the fort. When Union ships anchored outside the harbor on April 12, Confederate guns opened fire on Fort Sumter. The Civil War had begun. Soon Virginia, Arkansas, North Carolina, and Tennessee left the Union as well.

When Lincoln heard that the fort had surrendered, he asked for 75,000 militia volunteers. Across the North, men rushed to recruiting offices. But it seemed to take them forever to reach Washington. For more than a week, the capital was practically defenseless. Residents expected to be overrun by rebels at any moment. Lincoln, gazing out the

General Robert E. Lee, ✉ brilliant commander of the Confederate Army of Virginia.

✉ (opposite): The First Battle of Bull Run, July 21, 1861.

White House windows, murmured, "Why don't they come?"

Finally the first regiments arrived, marching down Pennsylvania Avenue with drums and bugles. For the rest of the spring and into the summer, Federals and Confederates trained, learning how to become soldiers. Then, in July, Union troops under General Irvin McDowell invaded Virginia, even though they were barely ready. They met the Confederates at a little creek called Bull Run. For inexperienced soldiers on both sides, the encounter was a dreadful revelation. So this was what fighting was like—the bombardment, the blood, the shrieks of horses, and the cries of men. For the North, which lost the battle, the effect was cataclysmic. This was going to be a real war after all. The day after Lincoln watched his demoralized troops retreat past his window at the White House, he called up another 500,000 troops.

Lincoln entrusted his new army to a handsome young general named George McClellan. "Little Mac," as his adoring troops called him, was vain, opinionated, and an excellent organizer. He found a group of raw, untrained farm boys "cowering on the banks of the Potomac" and turned them into a real army. But this dashing "Young Napoleon" had a chronic case of what the frustrated president called the "slows." No matter how much Lincoln urged him to get out and fight, McClellan made an excuse to delay. His troops were too raw. They were too tired. The enemy was too numerous. The horses had sores in their mouths. The truth was that McClellan liked his army and didn't want to see it hurt. As a result, he was cautious and indecisive.

The public grew impatient with the delays, and so did Lincoln. He began to study books on military strategy. As commander in chief, it was his duty to plan the war if his generals wouldn't.

McClellan's 100,000 troops trained throughout the fall of 1861 and winter of 1862. Then the general announced his plan to Lincoln: He

★ (opposite): An Army of the Potomac encampment during the Peninsular Campaign, spring 1862.

General George B. McClellan ⊠ was a cautious field commander, but he did transform the Army of the Potomac into a formidable fighting force.

Quick Facts

★ There were close to 3,000 Union troops killed, wounded, or missing at the First Battle of Bull Run. Confederate casualties were almost 2,000.

★ Lincoln appointed four of his main political rivals to his cabinet because he thought they were the best men for the job. They were initially resentful, but most came to trust and even revere the beleaguered president.

★ McClellan was openly contemptuous of Lincoln and his administration. He wrote to his wife, "The presdt. is nothing more than a well-meaning baboon. . . . It is sickening in the extreme . . . [to] see the weakness and unfitness of the poor beings who control the destinies of this great country." After he was dismissed as commander of the army, McClellan ran against Lincoln in the presidential election of 1864 and lost.

would attack Richmond, the Confederate capital, from the south. Slowly McClellan advanced his huge Army of the Potomac up the Virginia Peninsula between the James and York Rivers. He moved at such a snail's pace that Lincoln sent him a letter: "Dear General, if you do not want to use the army, I would like to borrow it for a few days."

When McClellan finally reached the outskirts of Richmond, he hesitated again. Due to erroneous spy reports, he was convinced the Confederate army was much larger than it was. While McClellan dawdled, General Robert E. Lee launched a surprise attack. In seven fierce battles, his Army of Northern Virginia pushed Union troops back down the peninsula. McClellan retreated back to Washington, D.C., boasting that he had "saved" the Army of the Potomac from destruction. The Union army suffered 16,000 casualties in the Peninsular Campaign. It would not even get near Richmond again for two years.

Lincoln had better luck in the Western arena. In Tennessee, a scrappy little man named Ulysses S. Grant captured two Confederate forts in February 1862. In April he won an even more important battle at Shiloh on the Tennessee River. However, the cost of the battle was so high—13,000 Union casualties—

that many people demanded that Lincoln dismiss Grant. But Lincoln said, "I can't spare this man. He fights."

Back in the East, Lee attacked Union troops at the Second Battle of Bull Run and defeated them. "Whipped again," Lincoln said, sighing. The war was going badly indeed.

The battlefield at Shiloh, April 1862. Shiloh was the most costly battle fought on North American soil up until that time. Worse battles were to come.

Chapter Four

The Lincoln White House

The Civil War began one month after Lincoln entered the White House and ended just five days before he died. While he inhabited the capital, it was an armed camp, crowded with soldiers, army hospitals, and supply depots. Pigs and chickens foraged in the muddy streets, and garbage floated in the gutters. Even the Capitol building was unfinished, its dome ringed by scaffolding. The White House itself was "ill-kept and dirty," according to Lincoln's secretary, John Nicolay. The two goats the Lincoln boys kept as pets made it even dirtier.

It was casual, too, particularly by today's standards. Lincoln, always informal, wandered through the halls at night dressed in his red flannel nightgown. Once, a congressman discovered him polishing his shoes. "Mr. Lincoln," he said, "gentlemen do not black their own boots." Lincoln shot back, "Whose boots do they black?" Washingtonians got used to the sight of the ungainly figure of their commander in chief strolling along Pennsylvania Avenue in the morning to pick up the newspaper. At 10:00 every morning he would receive visitors, ordinary Americans who wanted jobs, or favors, or a chat. In those days, practically anyone who wanted to see the president actually could. Lincoln called the receptions his "public opinion baths."

Lincoln was lucky that he could talk directly to the citizens because the press gave him a hard time. He was caricatured as a country bumpkin,

a coward, a crude jokester, and, by the Southern papers, as Satan him-self. Lincoln took the taunts in stride. "If the end brings me out right, what is said against me won't amount to anything," he pointed out. "If the end brings me out wrong, 10,000 angels swearing I was right won't make a difference."

Mary Lincoln was even more unpopular. Reporters criticized her extravagance, her Kentucky accent, and her presumably backwoods

⊠ Abraham Lincoln reading to his son Tad, February 9, 1864.

Willie Lincoln died in the White House at the age of 11.

manners. She was even suspected of being a traitor because many of her relatives were Confederate soldiers. What most people didn't know was that Mary visited the Washington hospitals regularly on a mission of mercy, bringing flowers and cheer to invalid soldiers. And despite her frequent temper tantrums—Mary was a very high-strung woman—she did her best to support her husband. Their love for each other remained strong.

Lincoln could always escape from the pressures of office by spending time with his sons. Willie, a sensitive boy who inherited his father's self-discipline, loved memorizing railroad tables. Mischievous Tad was very loving but had difficulty learning to read. Together, they tore through the White House corridors, playing soldier, building forts, and sailing ships. They sometimes burst into cabinet meetings unannounced. Their father enjoyed wrestling with them on Mrs. Lincoln's expensive Oriental carpets.

In February 1862, both boys fell ill with typhoid fever, probably from the polluted drinking water at the White House. Tad got well, but after two weeks of illness, Willie died. Lincoln was devastated. "We loved him so," he said. "It is hard, hard, to have him die." Mary Lincoln secluded herself for weeks and never really recovered.

Lincoln's love for his sons and grief for Willie gave him a special compassion for his soldiers. He used to go to the local hospitals and visit the wounded, both Union and Confederate. And, in those days of harsh martial law, he often recommended pardon for deserters, what he called his "leg cases": "Job Smith is not to be shot until further orders from me," he would write his generals. Or "I am appealed to in behalf of John Murphy, to be shot tomorrow. His mother says he is but 17.

Please answer." When a general complained of his leniency, Lincoln wrote, "Mr. General, there are already too many weeping widows in the United States. For God's sake, don't ask me to add to the number, for I won't do it."

Abolitionists in the North petitioned Lincoln to end slavery. Despite his personal feelings, Lincoln delayed. His duty as president, he thought, was to carry out the will of the American people, and most people were by no means sure they wanted emancipation. He explained himself in an open letter to the *New York Tribune*: "My paramount object in this struggle is to save the Union. . . . If I could save the Union without freeing any slave I would do that; and if I could save it by freeing some and leaving others alone I would also do that."

⊠ Black leader Frederick Douglass became acquainted with Lincoln during the war. He used his influence to urge Lincoln to free the slaves.

But as the war went on, more and more Northerners changed their minds. Yankee soldiers fighting in the South saw the horrors of slavery firsthand. Other soldiers began to understand that the best way to defeat the Confederates was to take away their means of support. Frederick Douglass wrote to Lincoln, "Arrest that hoe in the hands of the Negro, and you smite rebellion in the very seat of its life."

Finally it became apparent that freeing the slaves would indeed help save the Union. Lincoln prepared a draft of the Emancipation Proclamation. When he read it to his cabinet, Secretary of State William Henry Seward recommended that he not issue the proclamation until the North had won a big victory.

Soon Lincoln saw an opportunity. On September 17, 1862, the Confederates were defeated at Antietam Creek, Maryland, in the single bloodiest day of the war. Even though McClellan refused to pursue

Lee's retreating troops and obtain a more decisive victory, at least the Union didn't suffer a loss. Lincoln published his preliminary Emancipation Proclamation five days later. If the South didn't end their rebellion, he warned, "all persons held as slaves within any state or states, wherein the constitutional authority of the United States shall not then be practically recognized . . . shall then, thenceforward and forever, be free."

On January 1, 1863, Lincoln signed the final Emancipation Proclamation. When he put his pen down, he said, "If my name ever goes into history, it will be for this act."

Lincoln reading the first draft of the Emancipation Proclamation to his cabinet, July 22, 1862. After the proclamation was issued, black regiments started to be organized throughout the North.

Chapter Five

The Scourge of War

In the dark winter of 1863, Lincoln found himself under increased attack for the failure of his war. Morale was terrible, both in the army and on the home front. After dismissing George McClellan for the final time, Lincoln appointed bewhiskered Ambrose Burnside to command the Army of the Potomac. Burnside suffered a major defeat at Fredericksburg. Next, Lincoln tried Joseph Hooker, a boastful, handsome man who was a favorite of the troops. But Hooker seemed too confident. Lincoln had to remind his general that "the hen is the wisest of all the animal creation because she never cackles until the egg is laid."

Quick Facts

★ In March 1863, Congress instituted a national military draft. It called up all men between the ages of 20 and 45—except for those who could pay $300 to hire a substitute. The draft infuriated ordinary workers, who said it was a rich man's war and a poor man's fight.

★ The day after the Union won the Battle of Chattanooga on November 24, 1863, Lincoln called for a day of national prayer and thanksgiving. This became America's annual Thanksgiving Day.

★ In 1863, the painter Francis B. Carpenter came to the White House to prepare a painting of Lincoln reading the Emancipation Proclamation. He studied the president's face for months. "It was the saddest face I ever knew," Carpenter wrote later. "There were days when I could scarcely look into it without crying."

⊠ The last portrait ever taken of Lincoln, February 5, 1865. His worn face reveals the terrible toll the war has taken.

"The Mower" cartoon shows ⊠ Lincoln chopping up a "Copperhead" snake.

The "Peace Democrats" were Lincoln's major headache at home. They had many grievances: the horrific fatalities, the draft, the Emancipation Proclamation, and the enlistment of African Americans in the Union army. Republicans called the poisonous peaceniks "Copperheads." "You say you will not fight to free Negroes," Lincoln pointed out. "Some of them seem willing to fight for you."

Lincoln also had to deal with charges of tyranny. When the war started, he suspended the writ of habeas corpus so that citizens could be arrested and held without being told the reason. Secretary of War Edwin M. Stanton imprisoned as many as 15,000 people for opposing the war and endangering national security. When Lincoln was criticized for arresting an Ohio politician, he snapped, "Must I shoot a

⊠ (opposite): Action during the first day's fighting at Gettysburg, July 1, 1863.

Ulysses S. Grant, Lincoln's ⊠ most successful general.

simple-minded soldier boy who deserts, while I must not touch a hair of the wily agitator who induces him to desert?"

Then Lincoln's fears about the boastful Hooker came true. At the battle of Chancellorsville, from May 1 through May 4, General Lee demolished the Union troops in the greatest victory of his career. "My God! My God!" Lincoln moaned when he heard the news. "What will the country say?"

Encouraged by his success, Lee decided that the fastest way to end the war was to invade the North. A Confederate victory there would aid the cause of the Peace Democrats, and Lincoln might be forced to order a cease-fire. Two weeks after Lee crossed the Potomac, Lincoln replaced General Hooker with veteran George Gordon Meade. Three days later, from July 1 through July 3, Meade fought the bloodiest battle in American history. For three dreadful days, Union and Confederate forces clashed over a few miles of ground in the college town of Gettysburg, Pennsylvania. By the time the battle was over, 51,000 men had been lost on both sides—and the Confederate army was stumbling back to Virginia. The North had finally won a major victory.

More good news was on the way. Since the middle of May, General Grant had laid siege to Vicksburg, the last Confederate stronghold on the Mississippi River. A day after the battle of Gettysburg ended, Vicksburg surrendered.

Now Lincoln urged Meade to pursue the retreating Confederate army and destroy it. But Meade let Lee escape. Lincoln was distraught. As he told his son

General William Tecumseh Sherman ⊠

⊠ Abraham Lincoln, seated on the speaker's stand just before he delivered the Gettysburg Address. Lincoln is the bare-headed man to the left of the man with the top hat.

Robert, a God-given opportunity to end the war had been lost.

At least the tide of war had finally turned in the North's favor. And there was another consolation. The commander in chief had found a general who would fight. After McClellan let Lee get away in the wake of Antietam, a Washington poet pleaded, "Abraham Lincoln, give us a Man!" Lincoln had been disappointed with McDowell, McClellan, Pope, Burnside, Hooker, and Meade. On July 5 Lincoln declared, "Grant is my man, and I am his the rest of the war." Meanwhile, Grant and his friend General William Tecumseh Sherman continued to fight their way across Mississippi and Tennessee, trying to cut off the railroad lines leading to Richmond.

That fall Lincoln accepted an invitation to dedicate a new national cemetery at Gettysburg. The short speech he gave on November 19 may be the most famous of his career. The Gettysburg Address reflects Lincoln's conviction that the Civil War was nothing less than a test of democracy itself, fought so that "government of the people, by the people, for the people, shall not perish from the earth." He encouraged Americans to rededicate themselves to the ideals of the Declaration of

Independence and give to the nation "a new birth of freedom."

In February 1864, Lincoln invited Grant to come to Washington, D.C., to accept his new commission: lieutenant general, the highest rank in the U.S. Army. Lincoln took stock of his rumpled, unassuming general: "He's the quietest fellow you ever saw," Lincoln observed. "The only evidence you have that he's anyplace is that he makes things git! Wherever he is, things move!" Together, Grant and Lincoln devised their Grand Plan. Grant and the Army of the Potomac would keep after Lee in Virginia, pushing forward to Richmond. Meanwhile, General Sherman would drive toward the crucial railroad center of Atlanta, Georgia. No longer would Confederate armies be allowed to escape and regroup. Union troops would stay on the attack until the war was over.

Now some of the fiercest battles of the war took place: the

⊠ Sherman's men tearing up rails on the March to the Sea. After Union troops took Atlanta they marched through Georgia, destroying Confederate property in their path.

Wilderness, Spotsylvania, and Cold Harbor. The casualties were atrocious. In one month, Grant lost 50,000 men; Lee, some 32,000. From his White House windows, Lincoln could see thousands of wounded being transported to the Washington hospitals. Mary Lincoln echoed the feelings of the North when she wrote to her husband that Grant "is a butcher and is not fit to be head of an army." But Lincoln stood by his general. He wrote to Grant, "Hold on with bull-dog grip, and chew & choke, as much as possible."

For Lincoln, the summer of 1864 was the darkest time of the war. The country was tired of the struggle that would not end. Grant was stalled in Virginia. Sherman waited outside Atlanta. Radical Republicans thought Lincoln was too unpopular to win the election. Peace Democrats wanted the war to be over at any cost. Tired and heartsick though he was, Lincoln decided to run for office again for the good of the country. But it did not look as if he could win.

Then, suddenly, everything changed. On September 2, Sherman sent Lincoln a telegram: "Atlanta is ours, and fairly won." In Virginia, General Philip Sheridan beat Confederate forces in the Shenandoah Valley. In Alabama, Admiral David Farragut took Mobile Bay. The North took heart.

On November 8, 1864, Lincoln won 55 percent of the vote. It looked as though he would be president of the United States for another four years.

Chapter Six

Victory and Death

On March 4, 1865, Abraham Lincoln walked onto the podium for his second inaugural address. The completed Capitol dome rose behind him, surmounted by a statue of Liberty holding a sword and shield. Though it was a dank, drizzly day, the sun broke through the clouds as he began to speak. Many people took this as a good sign.

In his speech, Lincoln sounded the note of reconciliation and healing he hoped would lead the reunited nation in the years to come: "With malice toward none, with charity for all, with firmness in right, as God gives us to see the right, let us strive on to finish the work we are in; to bind up the nation's wounds, to care for him who shall have borne the battle, and for his widow, and his orphan—to do all which may achieve and cherish a just and lasting peace among ourselves, and with all nations."

Grant and Lee were still facing each other at Petersburg, 20 miles (32 km) south of Richmond. By late March, the dwindling Confederate troops, starving and exhausted, could no longer keep back the Federals. They had to retreat from Petersburg and abandon the defense of Richmond. Confederate president Jefferson Davis and the Confederate government fled from the capital, leaving it burned and ruined behind them. "Thank God I have lived to see this," Lincoln told a Union admiral. "It seems to me I have been dreaming a horrid dream for four years, and now the nightmare is gone. I want to see Richmond."

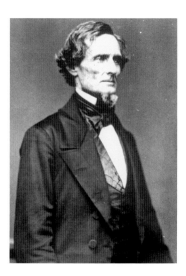

Confederate president Jefferson Davis fled Richmond on April 2. He was captured by Union troops on May 10, imprisoned for two years, and released without trial.

President Lincoln is greeted by former slaves when he enters Richmond on April 14, 1865.

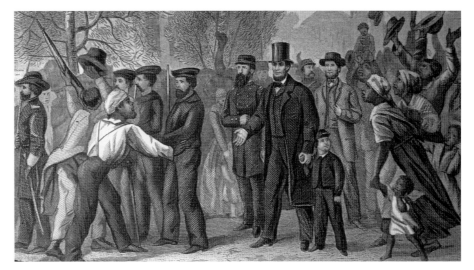

John Wilkes Booth, Shakespearean actor and murderer.

When Lincoln entered the silent, still-smoking city, hundreds of freed slaves came up to him, eager to see and touch "Father Abraham." When one black man fell to his knees to thank him, Lincoln said, "Don't kneel to me. That is not right. You must kneel to God only, and thank Him for the liberty you will enjoy hereafter."

At last, surrounded and out of supplies, Lee faced the inevitable. On April 9, he surrendered to General Grant at Appomattox Courthouse. Grant and Lincoln had already discussed the generous terms of surrender. Confederate soldiers, it was decided, would not be charged with treason. They could take their horses and go home. Already Lincoln was thinking about how best to accept the Southern states back into the nation. In a speech he gave before a joyous crowd in Washington the next day, he spoke of the difficulties of reconstruction. In passing, he mentioned the possible enfranchisement of blacks, specifically in Louisiana.

An actor named John Wilkes Booth was listening. He hated Lincoln and wanted revenge for the defeat of the Confederacy. "That is the last speech he will ever make," Booth snarled to a companion.

Quick Facts

- ★ Lincoln sponsored the Thirteenth Amendment to the Constitution, which Congress passed in January 1865. It abolished slavery within the United States. The amendment was ratified by the states on December 6, 1865.
- ★ Lincoln originally asked General Grant and his wife to accompany him to the theater on the night of April 14, but the Grants declined. Instead, he invited Major Henry Rathbone and his fiancée, Clara Harris. That night, John Wilkes Booth slashed at Rathbone with a knife. Rathbone's inability to protect the president eventually drove him mad. In 1894, he killed his wife because he was jealous of her love for their children. When he died in an insane asylum, his last words were: "The man with the knife! I can't stop him! I can't stop him!"
- ★ Tad Lincoln died of tuberculosis at age 18. Only Lincoln's oldest son, Robert, lived to become an adult. A successful lawyer and politician, he died in 1926.
- ★ Unhinged by grief, Mary Lincoln became progressively more eccentric until she finally died in 1882.

✉ (opposite): Lincoln's funeral procession marches down Pennsylvania Avenue in Washington, D.C.

Lincoln had always known he was in danger of being assassinated. "I long ago made up my mind that if anyone wants to kill me, he will do it," he once told a newspaper reporter. "If I wore a shirt of mail and kept myself surrounded by a bodyguard, it would be all the same."

That Friday, April 14, President and Mrs. Lincoln went to Ford's Theater in Washington to see a popular comedy called "Our American Cousin." Just as the audience erupted in the biggest laugh of the evening, Booth crept into the presidential box, placed his pistol behind Lincoln's left ear, and fired. Leaping down from the box, he caught his spur on an American flag and fell onto the stage, breaking his leg. Shouting *Sic semper tyrannis!*—"Thus ever to tyrants!"—he stumbled out of the theater. Twelve days later, trapped in a Virginia barn, Booth was killed by Federal cavalry troops.

Lincoln was mortally wounded. He was carried out of the theater to a boardinghouse across the street and laid diagonally across a too-small bed. There he died at 7:22 the next morning, watched by friends and family. The funeral was held in the East Room of the White House on April 19. Afterward, his funeral train traveled 1,600 miles (2,574 km) across the country, through towns and cities where mourners stood for hours to say goodbye. Vice President Andrew Johnson was sworn in as the 17th president of the United States.

Abraham Lincoln had been kind, generous, compassionate, strong, and determined when his country needed him most. If he had still been alive after the war, the North and South might have reconciled more easily, and Reconstruction might not have been so harsh. But we will never know. For by then, as Secretary of War Edwin Stanton said, Lincoln belonged to the ages.

Further Reading

Daugherty, James. *Abraham Lincoln*. New York: Viking Press, 1943.

Feinberg, Barbara Silberdick. *Abraham Lincoln's Gettysburg Address*. Brookfield, Conn.: Twenty-First Century Books, 2000.

Freedman, Russell. *Lincoln: A Photobiography*. New York: Clarion Books, 1987.

Hakim, Joy. *War, Terrible War: A History of Us*. New York: Oxford University Press, 1994.

Marrin, Albert. *Commander in Chief Abraham Lincoln and the Civil War*. New York: Dutton, 1997.

Meltzer, Milton, ed. *Lincoln in His Own Words*. San Diego: Harcourt Brace, 1993.

Glossary

Abolition—The act of abolishing, or getting rid of, slavery.

Amputation—The surgical removal of a limb or appendage.

Army of Northern Virginia—Confederate army stationed in Northern Virginia.

Army of the Potomac—Union army stationed along the banks of the Potomac River.

Casualty—A soldier who is killed, wounded, or missing.

Cavalry—The branch of an army that is mounted on horseback.

Confederate—A person who was a citizen of the Confederate States of America.

Confederate States of America—The name of the nation formed by the 11 states that seceded from the United States in 1860 and 1861.

Constitutional Convention (1787)—The meeting of delegates in Philadelphia who wrote a constitution for the United States.

Copperheads—Northerners who wanted to compromise with the Confederates and end the Civil War.

Emancipation Proclamation (1863)—President Lincoln's declaration freeing the slaves in the Confederacy.

Gettysburg Address (1863)—The speech given by President Lincoln after the Battle of Gettysburg.

Habeas Corpus—A citizen's right to a judicial hearing before being imprisoned.

Kansas-Nebraska Act (1854)—The law that divided Nebraska into two territories and stated that the question of slavery would be decided by popular sovereignty.

Militia—An army of citizens with no officially trained soldiers who serve during an emergency.

Missouri Compromise (1820)—A Congressional plan to keep the number of slave and free states equal.

Peace Democrats—Northern Democrats during the Civil War who wanted peace at any price.

Peninsular Campaign—Union general George B. McClellan's invasion of the Virginia Peninsula in the summer of 1862.

Popular Sovereignty—Before the Civil War, allowing each territory to decide for itself whether or not to allow slavery.

Radical Republicans—A group of Republicans in Congress who wanted to protect the rights of freedmen and punish former Confederates.

Reconstruction—The period after the Civil War when the former Confederate states were readmitted into the Union.

Regiment—A military unit of about 350 troops, usually commanded by a colonel.

Secede—To withdraw from or leave an organization.

Secessionist—In the Civil War, someone who believed in the right of a state to separate from the United States.

Shenandoah Valley Campaign—Confederate general Stonewall Jackson's campaign in Virginia's Shenandoah Valley.

Slavery—The state of one person being owned by another.

Union—During the Civil War, the states that did not secede from the United States of America.

Whig—The American political party formed in 1834 that was followed by the Republican Party.

Index